SPANISH COOKING

Rose Cantrell

WEATHERVANE BOOKS

contents

Introduction	4
Appetizers and Soups	5
Eggs	13
Salads	17
Vegetables	21
Fish and Seafood	29
Meats	39
Chicken	47
Breads	55
Desserts and Beverages	59

introduction

Spanish cuisine wears many hats, being influenced greatly by its colorful history and its harsh and varied terrain.

Since its colonization by Carthage in 500 BC, Spain has been occupied by the Celts, Romans, Vandals, Visigoths, and Moors. The Moors have probably had some of the most beneficial influences on the cuisine, as well as on the economic stabilization of the country. The Moors designed and built an irrigation system that today makes the coastal lands and southern hills a fertile valley that provides the luscious fruits and vegetables that are an integral part of the daily Spanish diet as well as a vital force in its economy.

Spain once colonized over half of the world. Spanish explorers returned to their homeland with such exotic new foods as corn, beans, chilies, chocolate, vanilla, tomatoes, eggplants, and potatoes. Today many of these foods can be found daily on a Spanish table.

Another factor influencing Spanish cuisine is the terrain. The country is divided into 47 provinces, for the most part physically separated by streams and hills. Because of these many physical barriers, the customs and heritage of the people and the climate of the province dictate the foods consumed by its people.

As a general rule the Southern provinces fry most of their food and depend on the sea for their daily meals. The Central land-locked region roasts the suckling pigs and tender young lambs that graze on the land. Northern provinces stew their food, because of the use of game and tough meats. The cold climate also lends to eating hearty dishes to remove the chill from the bones.

With all its differences, Spanish cooking has many common characteristics:

1) Common and almost exclusive use of olive oil as the source of fat for frying, baking, and cooking.

2) A lack of spices in their cooking. Although often thought to be like Mexican cooking, Spanish cuisine is mild. As a general rule the only spices used in cooking are saffron, paprika, salt, and cinnamon.

3) Use of garlic, onions, sweet green and/or sweet red peppers, and tomatoes cooked together in olive oil to make the basic sauce—*sofrito*.

4) Using chorizo (a garlic-flavored pork sausage) to add zest to recipes.

5) A lack of beef in their diet. Spain lacks the breed of cattle to produce a tender meat; far more important, they lack grazing land to support beef herds.

6) Extensive use of fish in their diet, taking advantage of their coastal location.

7) Using Serrano ham, a mountain smoked ham produced only in Spain, to flavor their food.

8) A lack of dairy products in their diet because grazing land will not support large herds.

As a rule Spanish people prefer to eat many meals rather than 3 large meals daily.

The first meal of the day is *desayuno* (breakfast). This is a light meal, consisting of a hot beverage and bread or pastry.

About 11 AM *almuerzo* (lunch) is eaten. This is usually a grilled meat or fish with a salad or omelet.

At 2:30 PM *comida* (dinner) is served. It consists of an appetizer, salad, vegetable(s), and a main dish. Dessert may or may not be served. After this meal Spaniards rest for 3 hours to allow the food to digest and to avoid the hot sun.

At 7:30 PM the shops close and it's time for *merienda* (snack). This is usually coffee and maybe a pastry.

Finally, at 10:00 to 11 PM the final meal or *cena* (supper) is eaten. It is usually a light meal similar to lunch.

However, if socializing in the cities of Spain, you may prefer to skip the *merienda* and *cena* and dine on the *tapas*—snacks that are served with your drinks.

The intent of this cookbook is to provide the reader and chef with a cross section of the cuisine found in all regions of Spain.

appetizers and soups

baby eels
anguilas

Because baby eels are available for such a short time each year, this dish is considered a great delicacy in Spain.

2 garlic cloves
⅔ cup olive oil
Dash of cayenne pepper
1 pound baby eels

Chop garlic cloves.

Heat oil in small skillet. Add garlic; sauté 2 to 3 minutes. Add cayenne.

Wash and drain eels. Add to oil; cook 30 seconds.

Serve eels hot. If used for a buffet, place on hot plate to keep warm. Makes 1 pint.

langostino with garlic mayonnaise
langostino con salsa ajo

A delicious summer dish served in Catalonia, the region known as ''All Things in Season'' because of its wide variety of fresh fruits, vegetables, and seafood.

3 cups cooked langostino
1 cup mayonnaise
½ teaspoon garlic powder

Cut langostino into bite-size pieces; chill.

Combine mayonnaise with garlic powder. (Use more or less garlic powder to taste.)

Place garlic mayonnaise in small bowl. Arrange cold langostino around garlic mayonnaise. Serve with cocktail picks for dipping. Makes 3 cups.

pickled fish
seviche

1 pound dressed freshly
  caught whitefish
1 cup lime juice, freshly
  squeezed
2 tomatoes
1 red pepper
1 green pepper

¼ cup pimiento-stuffed olives
2 tablespoons chopped onions
¼ cup olive oil
2 tablespoons wine vinegar
1 teaspoon oregano
1 teaspoon salt
½ cup slivered blanched olives

Wash fish well. Remove skin or bones; slice into small pieces. Place in small glass or stainless-steel bowl. Pour lime juice over fish; refrigerate 10 to 12 hours. Spoon juice over fish every 2 hours.

Peel and seed tomatoes; slice into thin wedges.

Core and seed peppers; slice into small strips.

Slice olives.

Add vegetables and remaining ingredients to fish 1 hour before serving time. Toss gently.

Serve fish arranged attractively on a platter with cocktail picks. Makes 8 servings.

pickled fish

pickled beets
remolachas escabache

A tapas served with mixed drinks.

1 teaspoon salt
½ teaspoon pepper
1 cup olive oil
¼ cup red-wine vinegar
½ tablespoon chopped onion
2 teaspoons parsley
1 teaspoon garlic juice
1 quart sliced beets, cooked

Combine all ingredients except beets in quart jar; shake until well-mixed. Pour over beets. Cover; marinate 24 hours in refrigerator. Toss occasionally to mix sauce and beets.

Serve as an appetizer or as a salad mixed with sweet onion rings. Makes 1 quart.

pickled cauliflower
coliflor escabache

2 quarts water
1 quart cider vinegar
½ cup noniodized salt
4 to 5 large heads cauliflower
1 tablespoon garlic powder
12 garlic cloves, peeled
24 dry red peppers
12 dill sprigs, dried

Combine water, vinegar, and salt in large saucepan; bring to boil. Clean cauliflower; break into florets. Soak in ice-cold water.*

Sterilize 12 pint jars. Put ¼ teaspoon garlic powder, 1 garlic clove, 2 peppers and 1 dill sprig in each jar. Fill each jar with cauliflower; cover to within ½ inch from top of jar with boiling vinegar mixture. Adjust lids. Process in boiling-water bath 15 minutes. Remove jars; cool slowly. Immediately use or reprocess jars that do not seal. Makes 12 pints.

* Cauliflower is soaked in ice cold water to retain its crispness when covered with the hot vinegar solution.

dates with ham
datiles con jamón

A delicious finger food.

16 pieces thinly sliced Serrano
  or other smoked ham
16 dates with pits removed

Wrap ham slices around dates. Arrange on serving platter. Makes 16 appetizers.

almond-stuffed olives
aceituna rellenos de almendra

24 whole almonds
24 large pitted green olives

Shell almonds. Drop into boiling water. Boil 2 to 3 minutes or until covering separates easily from almond meat.

For crisp almonds: Pull almond through hole in olive. Serve.

For soft almonds: Pull almond through hole in olive. Place stuffed olives back in olive juice; marinate at least 24 hours. Makes 24 stuffed olives.

chick-pea fritters
frityras de garbanzos

2 cups cooked chick-peas
¼ cup finely chopped onion
¼ teaspoon garlic powder
½ teaspoon baking powder
1 teaspoon salt

Dash of pepper
½ cup diced Serrano or other smoked ham
Olive oil for frying

Mash chick-peas with masher. Add remaining ingredients; mix well. Shape mixture into small balls. Press ham cube in center of each ball. Completely cover ham with dough.

Heat oil to 375°F. Deep-fat-fry balls until golden brown. Serve hot. Or heat oil in fondue pot. Arrange fritters around pot; allow guests to cook their own fritters. Makes 16 appetizers.

olive-ham turnovers

turnover pastry

2 cups flour
½ teaspoon salt
⅔ cup Garlic Mayonnaise (see Index)
Dash of cayenne
2 tablespoons cold water

turnover filling

⅔ cup ground Serrano or other smoked ham
⅔ cup chopped ripe olives
3 to 4 tablespoons mayonnaise

Heat oven to 425°F.

Sift flour with salt. Add mayonnaise, cayenne, and water; mix. Turn onto lightly floured board; roll thin. Cut into 2½-inch squares.

Mix together filling ingredients. Put generous ½ teaspoon filling on each pastry square. Moisten edges with water; fold over into triangles; pinch edges to seal. Bake 15 minutes or until pastry browns. Makes 2½ dozen turnovers.

tuna turnovers

Delicious tapas served in Madrid bars. Try them at your next party.

1 tablespoon chopped onion
1 3-ounce can mushrooms, drained (reserve liquid)
½ cup chopped pitted green olives
2 tablespoons butter

1 teaspoon flour
1 teaspoon garlic powder
¼ teaspoon salt
2 7-ounce cans tuna fish
1 package pie-crust mix

Sauté onion, mushrooms, and olives in butter. Stir in flour, garlic powder, salt, and mushroom liquid; heat. Add tuna.

Prepare pastry according to package directions. Roll out; cut into 2½-inch circles.

Place 2 teaspoons tuna mixture in center of each pastry circle. Fold pastry over. Dampen edges; seal. Bake in 450°F oven 7 minutes or until crust is golden brown. Makes about 2 dozen appetizers.

mild almond and pepper sauce
salsa romesca

1 cup Garlic Mayonnaise (see Index)
1 tablespoon lemon juice
2 tablespoons ground almonds
1 small tomato, peeled, seeded, chopped fine
Dash of cayenne*
¾ teaspoon anchovy paste

Combine ingredients in mixing bowl; mix well. Store in small covered jar in refrigerator. Makes 1¼ cups.

* For hot sauce, add 1 to 2 teaspoons cayenne.

chilindron sauce

¼ cup olive oil
1 garlic clove, chopped
1 onion, sliced into rings
1 green pepper, seeded, cut into strips
1 red pepper, seeded, cut into strips
Pinch of saffron
1 teaspoon salt
1 teaspoon paprika
Dash of cayenne*
1 cup diced Serrano or other smoked ham
1 tablespoon tomato paste
1½ cups tomato sauce

Heat oil in skillet. Add garlic; fry 10 minutes. Add onion and peppers; sauté until tender. Add remaining ingredients; bring to boil. Reduce heat; simmer 15 minutes.

Use as sauce for chicken, rabbit, or lamb. Makes about 2 cups.

* If hotter sauce is desired, use more cayenne.

garlic mayonnaise
ali-oli

1 egg
½ teaspoon salt
½ teaspoon garlic powder
Dash of cayenne pepper
1 cup olive oil
3 tablespoons fresh-squeezed lemon juice

Combine egg, salt, garlic powder, and ¼ cup oil in blender container. Blend thoroughly. With the blender running, very slowly add ½ cup oil. Gradually add lemon juice and remaining ¼ cup oil. Blend until thick. Occasionally scrape sides of bowl. Makes about 1 cup.

fried garlic croutons

1-pound loaf day-old bread
½ cup butter
¼ cup olive oil
1 teaspoon garlic powder
½ teaspoon salt
2 tablespoons dried parsley flakes

Cut bread into ½-inch cubes. Spread cubes evenly over cookie sheet. Let dry 2 days or until cubes lose moisture.

Heat butter and oil in large skillet until butter melts. Remove butter mixture from skillet; reserve. Add garlic powder, salt, and parsley to butter mixture; mix well.

Reheat skillet in which butter mixture was heated. Add croutons; distribute evenly over skillet surface. Pour butter mixture over croutons. Stir to distribute evenly. Fry croutons until golden brown and heated thoroughly. Cool; store up to 1 month in airtight container. Makes 2 quarts.

cheese mold
queso de cabrales

The main ingredient of this dish is a rare cheese ripened in the mountain caves of Asturias. The taste somewhat resembles blue cheese.

6 ounces *queso de cabrales* or blue cheese
¾ cup butter

Dash of cayenne
Ground pistachio nuts

Soften cheese; cream until smooth.

Cream butter until light and fluffy.

Blend together cheese, butter, and cayenne.

Line small mold with 3 layers cheesecloth, overlapping at top. Press cheese into mold. Cover top of cheese with overlapping cheesecloth. Refrigerate 24 hours.

Lift cheese out of mold, using cheesecloth. Turn onto serving dish. Carefully remove cheesecloth. Smooth rough edges with damp metal spatula. Sprinkle with pistachio nuts. Serve with vegetables and/or crackers. Makes 1½ cups.

almond soup
sopa de almendras

A food processor or blender makes this soup simple to prepare.

1½ cups almonds
1 garlic clove
2 cups water
1 cup white wine

2 tablespoons olive oil
½ teaspoon salt
White grapes
4 red-rose petals

Blanch almonds by dropping them into boiling water about 5 minutes or until outer shells come off easily.

Place almonds and garlic in food processor or blender; process until a meal develops. With machine running, gradually add water, wine, oil, and salt. Process until soup develops smooth consistency; chill.

Ladle soup into bowls; garnish with grapes and rose petals. Makes 4 servings.

bean and sausage soup
caldo gallego

By chilling the soup overnight, the flavors have a chance to blend.

1 pound dried white navy beans
1 pound chorizo or other garlic sausage
1 pound Serrano or other smoked ham, diced
1 ham bone
1 pound potatoes, diced

½ cup diced carrots
1 cup sliced leeks
4 cups chopped cabbage
1 clove garlic, pressed
1 bay leaf and 2 peppercorns tied together in cheesecloth
1 teaspoon salt
1½ quarts beef stock

Cover beans with water; soak overnight. Drain.

Combine beans with remaining ingredients in large pot; bring to boil. Reduce heat; simmer 4 to 6 hours or until beans and vegetables are tender. Remove sausage; skin and dice. Return to soup. Chill overnight.

Reheat soup to serve. Makes 20 servings.

cheese mold

garlic soup
sopa de ajo

In the traditional soup, only olive oil is used. However, the butter gives the soup a slightly milder taste.

⅓ cup olive oil
¼ cup butter
8 garlic cloves, peeled
½ teaspoon paprika
Dash of cayenne
1 teaspoon salt
¼ teaspoon pepper
3 cups bread cubes
6 cups boiling water

Heat oil and butter in deep cast-iron skillet until butter melts. Add garlic; sauté until golden brown. Remove garlic; mash. Reserve. Stir in spices. Add bread cubes. Fry until golden brown. Remove; save.

Add water to oil. Using a little water, form a paste with garlic. Add to soup; bring to boil. Reduce heat; simmer 30 minutes.

Ladle soup into serving bowls. Serve with bread cubes. Makes 8 servings.

Variation: Just prior to serving, beat 4 eggs. Slowly add to soup. Cook just long enough to set eggs.

gazpacho

gazpacho

The traditional Spanish soup.

**8 tomatoes, peeled, seeded,
chopped fine
1 cucumber, peeled, seeded,
chopped fine
1 cup finely chopped onions
1 sweet green pepper, seeded,
finely chopped
3 teaspoons salt
1 teaspoon garlic juice
¼ cup olive oil
¼ cup lemon juice
¼ teaspoon pepper
Dash of cayenne
2 cups tomato juice**

Combine tomatoes, cucumber, onions, and green pepper; mix well.
Sprinkle with salt. Let set at room temperature 1 hour to blend flavors.
Add remaining ingredients; mix well. Chill thoroughly.

Put ice cube in each serving glass. Fill with soup mixture. Serve with
Fried Garlic Croutons (see Index). Makes 6 to 8 servings.

quick gazpacho

**1 large cucumber
1 teaspoon salt
1 quart tomato juice
2 teaspoons onion juice
Dash of hot sauce
½ teaspoon Worcestershire
sauce**

**⅛ teaspoon white pepper
1 teaspoon sugar
1 tablespoon chopped fresh
parsley
Juice of 1 lemon
Fried Garlic Croutons (see
Index)**

Peel and dice cucumber. Sprinkle with ½ teaspoon salt. Squeeze with
your hands. Cover; let set 20 minutes. Drain.

Combine cucumbers with remaining ingredients, except croutons. Mix
thoroughly; chill thoroughly.

To serve, ladle into chilled soup cups; garnish with croutons. Makes 4
servings.

eggs

scrambled eggs
huevos revueltos

8 eggs
1 teaspoon salt
1 tomato, peeled, seeded, chopped
2 tablespoons olive oil
1 clove garlic, peeled
¼ cup chopped onions
½ cup chopped Serrano or other smoked ham
Chopped chives

Beat eggs with fork until frothy. Beat in salt.

Heat oil in shallow skillet. Add garlic; cook 5 minutes. Discard garlic. Add onions, tomato, and ham; sauté 5 minutes. Add eggs; cook, stirring frequently, until set.

Spoon eggs onto serving platter; garnish with chives. Makes 4 servings.

eggs with sofrito

omelet with sauce

14

eggs with sofrito
huevos con sofrito

½ cup olive oil
1 onion, peeled, chopped
1 garlic clove, peeled, minced
1 cup diced green pepper
2 large tomatoes, peeled,
  seeded, chopped
Dash of hot sauce
6 eggs
¼ cup grated Swiss cheese
¼ cup sliced pimiento-stuffed
  Spanish olives

Heat ¼ cup oil. Add onion, garlic, and pepper; sauté until tender. Add tomatoes; cook until mixture thickens. Stir in hot sauce.

Heat remaining ¼ cup oil in large shallow skillet. Crack eggs into skillet one at a time. Fry until whites set. Sprinkle with cheese. Cover; fry 2 minutes.

Put eggs on serving platter. Garnish with sofrito and olives. Makes 4 to 6 servings.

omelet with sauce
*tortilla de huevos
con salsa*

sauce

2 tablespoons olive oil
½ cup chopped onion
1 clove garlic, peeled,
  chopped
1 green pepper, cleaned,
  seeded, cut into strips
1 red pepper, cleaned, seeded,
  cut into strips
1 8-ounce can tomato sauce

Heat oil in small cast-iron skillet until haze forms over skillet. Add onion, garlic, and peppers; cook until vegetables begin to wilt. Add tomato sauce; heat thoroughly. Keep warm.

omelets

2 tablespoons olive oil
6 eggs
1 teaspoon salt
¼ teaspoon black pepper

Heat 1 tablespoon oil in small skillet or omelet pan.

Beat eggs until frothy. Beat in salt and pepper. Pour half of egg mixture into prepared pan; cook until set. Place omelet on warm serving plate. Cover half of omelet with sauce. Fold remaining half over top of sauce. Serve immediately. Prepare remaining omelet in same manner. Makes 4 servings.

onion and potato omelet

huevos con cebolla y papa

This omelet is often eaten cold in Spain, served between 2 pieces of thick bread.

¼ cup olive oil
1 large potato, washed, sliced thin
½ cup chopped onions

6 eggs
½ teaspoon salt
¼ teaspoon pepper

Heat 2 tablespoons oil in small shallow skillet. Add potato; sauté until tender. Add onions; sauté 2 minutes. Remove vegetables from skillet; drain.

Beat eggs until frothy. Add salt and pepper; mix well.

Heat 1 tablespoon oil in skillet. Add half of egg mixture. Using fork, poke holes in center of omelet to allow uncooked egg mixture to run under cooked omelet. Cook 1 minute or until outside rim of omelet is formed. Add half of potato and onion mixture. Flip omelet; cook 1 minute or until omelet is set. Repeat process with remaining egg and potato mixture. Makes 4 to 6 servings.

potato and sausage omelet

huevos con papa y salchicha

¼ pound garlic-flavored sausage
3 tablespoons olive oil
2 potatoes, peeled, sliced

½ cup diced green-onion tops
6 eggs, lightly beaten with fork
Salt and pepper to taste

Place sausage in small skillet; cover with water. Bring to boil; boil 5 minutes. Drain. Peel sausage; dice.

Heat oil in skillet. Add sausage and potatoes; fry until browned. Stir in onion; sauté until wilted. Remove sausage and vegetables. Add eggs to skillet. Sprinkle with meat and vegetables. Cook over low heat without stirring. As eggs set on bottom, lift edges and allow uncooked mixture to run underneath. Remove omelet from pan. Serve immediately. Makes 4 servings.

supper omelet

huevos de cena

A delicious late-night supper meal.

¼ cup olive oil
1 garlic clove, peeled
1 large onion, sliced into rings
1 green pepper, seeded, sliced into rings
1 red pepper, seeded, sliced into rings

1 tomato, peeled, seeded, sliced thin
1 large potato, peeled, sliced paper-thin
8 eggs
1 teaspoon salt
¼ teaspoon pepper

Heat 2 tablespoons oil in large shallow skillet. Add garlic; cook 5 minutes. Remove garlic; discard. Add onion and peppers; sauté until tender. Add tomato; sauté 3 to 4 minutes or until tomato begins to wilt but does not turn mushy. Remove vegetables from skillet. Keep warm.

Add remaining 2 tablespoons oil to skillet; heat. Add potato; fry until tender.

While potato is cooking, beat eggs, salt, and pepper until frothy. Add to potato. Cook until set. Do not flip.

Place omelet on serving plate; cover with cooked vegetables. To serve, cut into 4 wedges. Makes 4 servings.

salads

garbanzo bean salad
ensalada de garbanzo

A delicious salad in its own right or an ingredient in a tossed salad.

1 15-ounce can garbanzo
  beans, drained
¼ teaspoon garlic powder
2 tablespoons olive oil
2 tablespoons tarragon
  vinegar
¾ cup chopped celery

½ cup sliced pitted green
  olives
¼ cup chopped pimientos
3 scallions, chopped
½ teaspoon salt
Dash of pepper

Combine ingredients; mix well. Cover; marinate 24 hours in refrigerator.
Serve salad in lettuce cups. Makes 4 servings.

lettuce wedge with chunky tomato sauce
lechuga con salsa de tomate

1 head lettuce
2 tomatoes
¼ cup chopped green pepper
¼ cup chopped onion
2 tablespoons olive oil
1 tablespoon lemon juice

¼ teaspoon garlic powder
½ teaspoon crushed coriander
  leaves
½ teaspoon salt
Dash of cayenne

Core head of lettuce; cut into 6 wedges.

Peel, seed, and chop tomatoes.

Combine all ingredients except lettuce. Beat with electric mixer on low speed 3 to 4 minutes or until tomatoes start to form their own juice. Let stand in refrigerator 3 hours to allow flavors to combine before serving.

To serve, place lettuce wedge on salad plate. Pour tomato sauce over wedge. Makes 6 servings.

mixed salad
ensalada mixta

2 cucumbers, peeled, sliced into rings
1 dozen small tomatoes, sliced into circles
1 green pepper, seeded, sliced into strips
1 red pepper, seeded, sliced into strips
1 Spanish onion, peeled, cut into rings

Combine all ingredients; toss lightly.

Arrange salad on individual serving plates. Top each salad with 2 tablespoons dressing. Makes 4 servings.

salad dressing

¼ cup olive oil
3 tablespoons wine vinegar
½ teaspoon salt
¼ teaspoon white pepper
1 teaspoon garlic juice
¼ teaspoon crushed oregano
1 tablespoon chopped fresh parsley

Combine all ingredients; mix well.

scalded salad

2 cups shredded leaf lettuce
1 onion, peeled, sliced into thin rings
1 green pepper, seeded, sliced into thin rings
5 bacon slices
Dash of garlic powder
Salt and pepper to taste

Toss lettuce, onion, and green pepper together.

Dice bacon. Fry until crisp. Remove bacon with slotted spoon. Add spices to hot bacon grease. Pour hot grease over salad greens, tossing as you pour. Sprinkle with bacon pieces. Serve immediately. Makes 4 to 6 servings.

tossed salad
ensalada tirara

½ head iceberg lettuce
1 tomato
1 green pepper
¼ cup pitted green olives
2 celery stalks
5 radishes
½ cup canned tuna fish
1 can anchovies
6 canned sardines

Tear lettuce into bite-size pieces.

Slice tomato and pepper into thin strips.

Slice olives.

Dice celery.

Cut radishes into slices.

Place vegetables and tuna fish into large bowl; toss gently.

Fill 6 individual salad bowls with tossed salad. Garnish each salad with anchovies and sardines. Pour dressing over individual salads or pass and let guests pour their own. Makes 6 servings.

salad dressing

¼ cup olive oil
2 tablespoons lemon juice
¾ teaspoon salt
¼ teaspoon pepper
1 teaspoon oregano
¼ teaspoon garlic powder

Combine ingredients; mix well.

fresh-fruit salad
ensalada de frutas freso

1 fresh pineapple
2 oranges
½ Spanish melon
1 pound green seedless grapes
2 Delicious apples

Peel pineapple. Cut into ¾-inch slices; remove rind and eyes. Cut into cubes, discarding center core.

Peel and section oranges.

Remove seeds from melon; slice into wedges.

Wash grapes; remove from stems. Slice in half.

Peel and dice apples.

Gently mix fruit in large bowl.

Serve salad with Honey Dressing on the side. Makes 8 to 10 servings.

honey dressing

¾ cup mayonnaise
⅓ cup honey
¼ cup orange juice
⅛ teaspoon grated onion

Combine ingredients; mix well.

fresh-fruit salad

melon salad

melon salad
ensalada de tlacopan

A refreshing Spanish salad using an orange from the region of Valencia, a melon from Madrid, and strawberries from Callella.

1 Spanish melon
1 cup fresh strawberries
1 orange
2 tablespoons honey
½ cup whipped cream
Pistachio nuts

Slice ¼ of top off melon; remove seeds. Scoop meat from melon, using melon-ball scoop; save melon shell. Place balls in large bowl.

Wash and remove stems from strawberries. Add to melon balls.

Peel orange; slice into sections by cutting between membranes. Add to melon balls.

Drizzle honey over fruit. Toss gently.

Fill melon shell with honeyed fruit. Garnish with whipped cream and pistachio nuts; chill. Makes 4 to 6 servings.

poached oranges

This dish is served in place of a salad in the height of the orange season.

4 oranges
1 cup sugar
½ cup sherry

Peel and remove all white membrane from oranges. Place oranges in saucepan; cover with water. Bring to boil. Reduce heat; simmer 15 minutes. Remove from water. Add sugar to water. Bring to slow boil; boil until thin syrup forms. Place oranges in syrup; simmer 5 minutes. Remove oranges from syrup; drizzle with wine.

Chill oranges before serving. Makes 4 servings.

vegetables

green beans with ham
habas con jamón

2 tablespoons olive oil
1 Spanish onion, chopped
2 10-ounce packages frozen
   green beans
½ teaspoon garlic juice

½ teaspoon salt
1 cup diced Serrano or other
   smoked ham
Pimiento

Heat oil until light haze forms above pan. Reduce heat; sauté onion and beans until tender. Add garlic juice, salt, and ham; cook 5 minutes or until ham is heated.

Serve beans and ham warm, garnished with pimiento. Makes 6 servings.

green beans in tomato sauce
habas en salsa de tomate

3 tablespoons olive oil
½ cup chopped Spanish onion
1 clove garlic, minced
1 pound fresh green beans,
   washed, tips removed
1 16-ounce can stewed
   tomatoes

1 tablespoon tomato paste
½ teaspoon salt
Dash of pepper
1 teaspoon sugar
1 tablespoon parsley

Heat oil in deep cast-iron skillet. Sauté onion and garlic until golden brown. Add remaining ingredients. Cover; cook 30 minutes or until beans are fork-tender. Remove beans. Cook tomato sauce until almost all liquid evaporates. Re-add beans to sauce; reheat. Makes 6 servings.

steamed white asparagus with garlic mayonnaise
espárrago blanco vapora con salsa ajo

White asparagus are grown under mounds of dirt to prevent the chlorophyll in the spears from turning green.

2 pounds white asparagus
⅓ cup olive oil or butter
⅔ cup water
1 teaspoon salt
Garlic Mayonnaise (see Index)

Break off each asparagus spear as far as it will snap easily; peel off scales with potato peeler. Rinse several times to remove sand.

Heat oil and water to boiling in pan large enough to accommodate asparagus stalks. Add asparagus and salt to boiling water; cover pan. Cook over high heat 12 minutes or until asparagus is fork-tender; drain.

Serve asparagus immediately with Garlic Mayonnaise. Makes 6 servings.

lima beans and peppers
habas verdes y pimientos

¾ cup water
1 10-ounce package frozen lima beans
3 tablespoons olive oil
½ cup thin strips green pepper
½ cup thin strips red pepper
¼ cup chopped onion

Bring water to boil. Add beans; cook 10 minutes or until tender. Drain; keep warm.

Heat oil in skillet. Add remaining vegetables; sauté 5 minutes.

Combine beans with vegetables. Serve immediately. Makes 4 servings.

cabbage with apples
col con manzanas

1 small head cabbage
1 cooking apple
2 tablespoons olive oil or bacon drippings
1 teaspoon caraway seed
1 cup dry white wine
½ teaspoon salt
¼ teaspoon pepper
Lemon wedges

Core and shred cabbage.

Peel, core, and coarsely grate apple.

Pour oil into large skillet. Add cabbage; sauté 10 minutes. Add apple, caraway seed, and wine. Cover; simmer 10 minutes or until cabbage is tender. Season with salt and pepper. Serve with lemon wedges. Makes 4 to 6 servings.

Picture on opposite page: steamed white asparagus with garlic mayonnaise

onions and green peppers
cebollas y pimientos verde

¼ cup olive oil
6 medium onions, peeled, sliced thin
3 green peppers, seeded, sliced into thin rings
½ teaspoon salt
¼ teaspoon pepper

Heat oil in skillet; sauté onions 10 minutes. Add peppers; sauté 10 minutes or until tender. Sprinkle with salt and pepper. Makes 4 servings.

boiled potatoes with garlic mayonnaise
papas hervira con salsa ajo

2 pounds new potatoes
1 teaspoon salt
1 recipe Garlic Mayonnaise (see Index)
1 tablespoon snipped fresh parsley

Scrape skin from potatoes.* Cut large potatoes in two. Cover with water. Add salt; bring to boil. Boil 20 minutes or until tender; drain.

Prepare mayonnaise as directed.

Toss potatoes in mayonnaise; garnish with parsley. Serve hot. Makes 6 to 8 servings.

* Use paring knife, not potato peeler. Skins of new potatoes are too thin to remove with peeler.

potatoes with parsley

1 to 1½ pounds new potatoes
1 cup water
1 teaspoon salt
⅓ cup olive oil or melted butter
1 tablespoon snipped fresh parsley flakes

With paring knife, scrape skins from new potatoes.*

Bring water and salt to rolling boil. Add potatoes; cover. Simmer 20 minutes or until fork-tender; drain.

Heat oil.

Pour potatoes into serving bowl. Coat with hot oil; sprinkle with parsley. Makes 4 servings.

* Do not use potato peeler. Skins of new potatoes are too thin to remove with peeler.

spanish rice
arroz de español

3 tablespoons olive oil
1 garlic clove, crushed
1 small onion, chopped
½ cup chopped red pepper
1 cup long-grain rice
1 teaspoon salt
2 cups boiling chicken stock
2 tomatoes
1 cup frozen peas

Heat oil in large skillet until haze begins to form. Add garlic, onion, and pepper; sauté until vegetables are limp. Add rice; be sure it is well-coated with oil and turns opaque. Add salt and chicken stock. Bring to boil; cover. Reduce heat; simmer 30 minutes or until liquid is absorbed by rice.

Peel, seed, and dice tomatoes. Add tomatoes and peas to rice; stir. Cook just long enough to heat peas and tomatoes. Makes 6 servings.

summer garden casserole
cazuelo de jardín verano

A Spanish housewife combines the abundance of her garden for a summer vegetable treat.

3 summer squash, sliced
2 potatoes, peeled, sliced
2 carrots, peeled, sliced
2 medium onions, peeled, sliced
2 cups chopped peeled tomatoes
2 garlic cloves, minced
½ cup olive oil
¼ cup snipped parsley
¾ teaspoon salt
¼ teaspoon pepper

Oil large casserole; layer ¼ of squash, potatoes, carrots, and onions. Combine tomatoes and garlic. Put ¼ of tomato mixture, 2 tablespoons oil, 1 tablespoon parsley, and some of salt and pepper over vegetables. Repeat until all vegetables are layered. Cover; bake at 350°F 1 hour or until tender. Makes 4 to 6 servings.

pepper pot
pote de pimiento

2 red sweet peppers
2 green peppers
1 large Spanish onion
3 large tomatoes
¼ cup olive oil
1 teaspoon salt
½ teaspoon garlic powder
¼ teaspoon pepper

Remove tops, seeds, and white membranes from peppers. Slice into rings.

Peel onion; slice into rings.

Peel tomatoes. Remove cores; slice into wedges.

Heat oil in large skillet; reduce heat. Add peppers and onion; sauté 10 minutes. Add tomatoes and seasonings. Sauté 10 minutes or until vegetables are tender but still retain their shape. Makes 4 servings.

hominy soup
pozole

1 leftover ham bone
1 stewing chicken, cut up
2 onions, chopped
2 garlic cloves, chopped fine
2¾ quarts water
1 tablespoon salt
3 peppercorns
2 bay leaves
1 pound leftover ham, cubed
1 29-ounce can white hominy

Combine ham bone, chicken, onions, garlic, water, and spices in soup kettle; bring to boil. Reduce heat; simmer 2 hours. Add ham and hominy with liquid; cook 1 hour. Remove meat, peppercorns, and bay leaf from soup.

Remove meat from bones; re-add to soup. Refrigerate overnight to blend flavors.

To serve, remove soup from refrigerator. Skim fat; reheat. Makes 8 to 10 servings.

saffron rice

3 tablespoons olive oil
1 green pepper, chopped
1 red pepper, chopped
½ cup chopped Spanish onion
1 cup long-grain rice
1 teaspoon garlic powder
⅛ teaspoon saffron
2 cups chicken broth

Heat oil in skillet. Add peppers and onion; sauté until wilted. Add rice; cook until opaque. Add remaining ingredients. Bring mixture to boil; cover. Reduce heat; simmer 30 minutes or until liquid is absorbed by rice. Makes 4 to 6 servings.

pepper pot

saffron rice

boiled shrimp with sauces

fish and seafood

boiled shrimp with sauces
camarón herviro con salsas

This dish can be served as an appetizer or main course.

2 quarts water
Dash of hot sauce
5 peppercorns
1 lemon, sliced
2 teaspoons salt
1 garlic clove, peeled
2 bay leaves
1 onion, quartered
1 celery heart
**3 pounds fresh medium
   shrimp**
Garlic Mayonnaise (see Index)
**Almond and Pepper Sauce
   (see Index)**

Bring water to boil. Add hot sauce, peppercorns, lemon, salt, garlic, bay leaves, onion, and celery. Boil 10 minutes. Add shrimp. Bring water back to boil. Cook shrimp 6 to 8 minutes. Cover; remove from heat. Let stand 15 minutes; drain.

Peel and devein shrimp; chill.

Prepare sauces as directed in recipes.

Place shrimp on serving platter. Serve with sauces, large salad, and Continental Bread (see Index). Makes 6 servings or appetizers for 12.

galician steamed fish in tomato sauce

pescado vaporo en salsa tamate de galicia

2 pounds whitefish fillets
1 small onion, peeled,
 quartered
1 bay leaf
2 tablespoons olive oil
1 garlic clove, minced
½ cup chopped onion
6 medium tomatoes, peeled,
 seeded, chopped
1 teaspoon paprika
Dash of cayenne
1 teaspoon chopped chives
⅓ cup white wine
Vinegar

Place fish, quartered onion, and bay leaf on large piece of aluminum foil. Securely close foil. Place fish in steamer; steam 25 minutes or until fish flakes easily.

Heat oil in deep skillet. Add garlic and chopped onion; sauté until tender. Add tomatoes, paprika, cayenne, chives, and wine. Simmer 30 minutes.

Place fish on serving platter; top with tomato sauce. Serve with vinegar. Makes 4 to 6 servings.

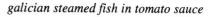

galician steamed fish in tomato sauce

cod bake

2 tablespoons olive oil
1 Spanish onion, chopped
1 green pepper, peeled,
    seeded, chopped
1 cup sliced fresh mushroom

1 garlic clove, minced
1 bay leaf
1 16-ounce can stewed
    tomatoes
1½ pounds cod fillets

Heat oil until haze forms above skillet. Add onion, pepper, mushroom, and garlic; sauté until limp. Add bay leaf and tomatoes; simmer 30 minutes. Remove bay leaf.

Arrange cod in greased baking dish. Pour sauce over cod. Bake in 350°F oven 40 minutes or until fish flakes easily. Makes 4 servings.

baked fresh sardines
sardinas frescas al horno

3 pounds sardines, dressed
1 teaspoon salt
½ teaspoon pepper
2 tablespoons olive oil
2 Spanish onions, peeled,
    sliced thin
2 large tomatoes, peeled,
    sliced

1 green pepper, seeds
    removed, sliced into rings
3 tablespoons chopped chives
⅓ cup dry white wine
6 large lettuce leaves (Use the
    outer leaves that you
    generally throw away.)

Pat fish dry. Sprinkle with salt and pepper.

Grease large casserole with oil. Arrange onions in layers on bottom of casserole. Layer fish over onions. Cover fish with tomato slices and pepper rings. Sprinkle with chives. Pour wine over fish and vegetables. Cover dish with lettuce leaves. Marinate in refrigerator 6 hours. Bake, covered, in 375°F oven 30 minutes or until fish flakes easily. Remove lettuce leaves; discard. Bake 10 minutes. Makes 6 servings.

tuna fish with rice salad
atum con ensalada arroz

2 7-ounce cans tuna fish,
    drained
2 cups cooked rice
2 green peppers, seeds
    removed, chopped
2 tomatoes, peeled, seeded,
    chopped
1 small onion, peeled,
    chopped

¾ cup Garlic Mayonnaise (see
    Index)
1 tablespoon dry mustard
4 large lettuce leaves
2 hard-cooked eggs, sliced
½ cup pitted black olives

Combine tuna, rice, peppers, tomatoes, and onion.

Combine mayonnaise and mustard; mix well. Add to tuna mixture; toss. Chill salad thoroughly.

Place lettuce leaves in bottom of serving bowl. Lightly spoon salad over lettuce. Garnish with egg slices and olives. Makes 4 to 6 servings.

tuna stew
marmitako

2 tablespoons olive oil
1 medium onion, chopped
1 teaspoon garlic powder
2 tablespoons parsley flakes
1 1-pound can stewed
  tomatoes
2 large potatoes, diced
1 beef bouillon cube
1 cup frozen peas
½ cup diced red pepper
1 bay leaf
1 teaspoon salt
½ teaspoon pepper
2 6½-ounce cans tuna

Heat oil in large skillet. Add onion; sauté until transparent. Add remaining ingredients, except tuna; stir to mix. Cover; simmer ½ hour or until potatoes are tender. Add tuna; mix well. Simmer 10 minutes to heat tuna thoroughly.

Serve tuna with rice or toast. Makes 4 servings.

fried fish with sour sauce
escabeche de pescado frito

1 pound firm whitefish fillets
¾ teaspoon salt
1 Spanish onion, sliced
½ cup olive oil
1 clove garlic, minced
½ cup water
1 bay leaf
6 whole peppercorns
½ teaspoon toasted coriander
  seeds
1 egg, well-beaten
2 tablespoons water
¾ cup flour
½ cup vinegar
3 tablespoons olive oil
⅓ cup sliced pimiento-stuffed
  Spanish olives
¼ cup chopped onion

Sprinkle fish with salt; let stand ½ hour.

Slowly fry sliced onion in ½ cup oil in cast-iron frying pan. Add garlic; fry 3 minutes. (Do not brown.) Remove onion and garlic from oil with slotted spoon; place in saucepan. Add ½ cup water, bay leaf, peppercorns, and coriander; simmer while frying fish.

Beat egg and 2 tablespoons water together. Dip fish in egg wash, then in flour. Fry in seasoned oil until golden brown. Drain on brown paper bag.

Add vinegar and 3 tablespoons oil to onion and spice mixture. Remove bay leaf, peppercorns, and coriander seeds.

Pour sauce over fish; garnish with olives and chopped onion. Makes 4 servings.

andalusia daily soup

sopa diario de andalusia

This fish soup gets its name from the fact that Andalusian housewives make soup from their husbands' daily catch at sea.

3 pounds assorted fish
¼ cup olive oil
2 garlic cloves, peeled,
  chopped
1 onion, peeled, chopped
1½ quarts water
2 peppercorns
1 bay leaf
Dash of cayenne
Lemon slices

Clean and dress fish. Cut into bite-size pieces. Scrub mussels, if used, and soak in cold water 20 minutes to remove excess salt.

Heat oil in large Dutch oven; sauté garlic and onion 10 minutes. Add all fish but shellfish, water, peppercorns, bay leaf, and cayenne. Cover; simmer 15 minutes or until fish flakes easily. Remove fish from stock; remove skin and bones. Add fish meat back to stock, along with any shellfish used. Cook 7 to 10 minutes or until shellfish are done. Remove peppercorns and bay leaf. Serve with lemon slices. Makes 6 servings.

broiled fish

A vendor broiling fish along the harbor is a familiar scene in Spanish seaports.

6 dressed whole fish
2 teaspoons salt
Dash of cayenne (optional)
3 tablespoons olive oil
3 tablespoons freshly squeezed
  lemon juice
Fresh parsley sprigs, snipped
1 recipe Almond and Pepper
  Sauce (see Index)
1 recipe Garlic Mayonnaise
  (see Index)

Wash and drain fish. Scrape scales.

Combine salt, cayenne, oil, and lemon juice; mix well. Baste fish with sauce. Let marinate 2 hours in refrigerator or on crushed ice.

Place fish over hot coals; grill 10 minutes. Turn fish; grill 10 minutes or until fish flakes easily. Remove to serving platter; sprinkle with parsley.

Prepare sauces as directed; serve with fish. Makes 6 servings.

seafood and rice
paella la mancha

4 chicken breasts
¼ cup olive oil
1 cup chicken stock
2 tablespoons olive oil
½ cup chopped Spanish onion
1 clove garlic, minced
1¼ cups raw long-grain rice
¼ cup white wine
⅛ teaspoon saffron
Dash of cayenne pepper

1 teaspoon salt
2 cups chicken broth
1 1-pound can cooking
  tomatoes, drained
½ cup chopped Serrano or
  smoked ham
12 fresh shrimp, peeled,
  deveined
1 cup frozen peas
1 cup frozen green beans

Wash chicken; pat dry. Cut breast in half; de-bone if desired.

Heat ¼ cup oil in skillet; sauté chicken until well-browned on all sides. Add 1 cup chicken stock. Reduce heat; simmer, covered, 20 minutes. Set chicken aside. Save pan juices.

Heat 2 tablespoons oil in Dutch oven. Sauté onion and garlic until limp. Add rice; sauté until lightly browned. Add pan juices, wine, spices, 2 cups chicken broth, drained tomatoes, ham, and shrimp to Dutch oven. Stir well. Cover; bring to boil. Reduce heat to low; cook 25 minutes. Add vegetables; cook 10 minutes. Makes 6 servings.

shrimp with vegetables
camarón con legumbres

A delightful dish for a backyard buffet.

2 15-ounce cans artichoke
  hearts
1 small head cauliflower
1½ cups olive oil
½ cup vinegar
¼ cup dry white wine
1 tablespoon sugar
1 teaspoon garlic juice
4 teaspoons salt

Dash of cayenne
½ teaspoon dry mustard
1½ quarts water
5 peppercorns
½ lemon, sliced
1 bay leaf
1 onion, peeled, quartered
1½ pounds fresh medium
  shrimp

Drain artichoke hearts.

Select saucepan large enough to accommodate head of cauliflower. Cover bottom of pan with 1 to 2 inches water. Add salt to water; bring to rapid boil. Add cauliflower to saucepan; cover. Cook 25 minutes or until fork-tender. Drain immediately; cool. Break into florets.

Combine oil, vinegar, wine, sugar, garlic juice, 2 teaspoons salt, cayenne, and mustard in jar. Cover; shake vigorously. Pour vinegar and oil mixture over vegetables. Cover; marinate in refrigerator overnight.

Bring water to boil. Add peppercorns, lemon, 2 teaspoons salt, bay leaf, and onion; boil 10 minutes. Add shrimp; bring water back to boil. Cook shrimp 6 to 8 minutes. Cover; remove from heat. Let stand 15 minutes; drain. Peel and devein shrimp; chill.

Add shrimp to marinating vegetables first thing in morning. Re-cover. Return mixture to refrigerator; marinate at least 6 hours prior to serving. Drain before serving. Makes 6 to 8 servings.

shrimp and lobster salad
ensalada de camerón et langosta

1½ cups cooked lobster meat
1½ cups cooked shrimp
½ cup chopped Spanish onion
2 tablespoons olive oil
2 tablespoons lemon juice
4 tomatoes
2 hard-cooked eggs
Lettuce leaves
Lemon wedges
1 recipe Garlic Mayonnaise
   (see Index)

Combine lobster, shrimp, onion, oil, and lemon juice; mix well. Refrigerate until ready to use.

Slice tomatoes and eggs.

Arrange lettuce leaves on 4 plates.

Place 1 sliced tomato on each lettuce leaf. Top tomatoes with seafood salad. Garnish with hard-cooked egg slices and lemon wedges. Serve with Garlic Mayonnaise. Makes 4 servings.

baked fish
pescado al horno

Spanish cooking uses only olive oil. If you find the olive oil taste too strong, butter can be substituted to prepare the bread crumbs.

3 pounds hake, haddock, or
   cod fillets
1 teaspoon salt
½ teaspoon pepper
Dash of cayenne pepper
1 tablespoon olive oil
2 Spanish onions, peeled,
   sliced thin
2 large tomatoes, peeled,
   sliced

2 tablespoons chopped
   pimiento
1 Valencia orange, sliced
12 fresh mushrooms, cleaned,
   sliced
3 tablespoons chopped chives
⅓ cup white wine
½ cup olive oil or butter,
   melted
1¼ cups fresh bread crumbs

Pat fish dry with paper towel.

Combine salt, pepper, and cayenne. Sprinkle mixture over fish.

Grease large baking dish with 1 tablespoon oil. Arrange onions in layers on bottom of dish. Layer fish over onions. Cover fish with tomato slices, pimiento, and orange slices. Layer mushrooms around fish. Sprinkle with chives. Pour wine over fish and vegetables. Cover with foil; marinate in refrigerator 6 to 8 hours. Bake, covered, in 375°F oven 25 to 30 minutes or until fish flakes easily. Uncover.

Combine ½ cup oil and bread crumbs. Sprinkle fish with bread crumbs. Bake 5 to 10 minutes or until browned. Makes 6 servings.

Picture on following pages: baked fish

meats

marinated beef roast
carne de vaca asada

1 teaspoon garlic juice
½ teaspoon freshly ground
   black pepper
1 bay leaf
2 whole cloves
1½ cups dry red wine

1 4- to 6-pound rolled beef
   roast
3 tablespoons olive oil
2 tablespoons flour
2 tablespoons water

Combine garlic juice, pepper, bay leaf, cloves, and wine in large roaster. Add roast. Spoon mixture over roast. Cover; marinate overnight in refrigerator, occasionally basting roast with marinade.

Heat oil in large skillet.

Remove roast from marinade; pat dry. Brown on all sides. Place roast back into marinade. Cover; bake in 375°F oven 2 hours. Uncover; allow roast to brown about 30 minutes. Remove roast from pan.

Place roasting pan with marinade on burner. Bring to boil.

Make paste with flour and water; pour into marinade, stirring constantly. Cook until thickened.

Slice roast; serve with gravy. Makes 4 to 6 servings.

beef simmered in wine
carne de vaca en vino

4 2-inch-thick filets mignons
1 teaspoon salt
½ teaspoon peppermill-
   ground black pepper

½ cup olive oil
1 large Spanish onion, peeled,
   sliced into rings
1 cup dry red wine

Rub filets mignons with salt and pepper.

Heat oil in heavy frying pan. Add steaks; brown on both sides. Reduce heat to simmer. Add onions and wine. Cover skillet tightly; simmer steaks 30 minutes. Makes 4 servings.

Picture on opposite page: marinated beef roast

marinated lamb chops

In almost every Spanish fishing port, you will find meat and fish being grilled in the open air.

2 cups dry red wine
2 tablespoons olive oil
2 tablespoons minced garlic
½ cup chopped onion
1 bay leaf
½ teaspoon salt
Dash of pepper
8 lamb chops, 1½ to 2 inches
   thick

Combine all ingredients except lamb; mix well. Pour marinade over chops. Cover; refrigerate overnight. Turn meat occasionally. Remove chops from marinade; grill over hot coals until desired doneness. Turn once during cooking process. Makes 4 servings.

spanish lamb chops
chuletas de carnero español

¼ cup olive oil
3 tablespoons lime juice
1 garlic clove, crushed
2 tablespoons grated onion
½ teaspoon salt
⅛ teaspoon pepper
4 1-inch-thick lamb chops

Combine oil, lime juice, garlic, onion, salt, and pepper; mix well. Pour mixture over lamb chops; refrigerate. Marinate 24 hours.

Grill chops over hot coals, about 12 minutes per side. Brush chops with marinade while cooking.

Heat remaining marinade; serve with chops. Makes 4 servings.

pork rolls
rollos de carne de cerdo

An accompaniment for a cocido or a delicious dish in its own right.

1 pound lean pork, ground
   once
¼ teaspoon pepper
1½ teaspoons garlic powder
1 teaspoon salt
1 egg, beaten
1 tablespoon parsley
1 cup soft bread crumbs
   (about)
1 cup flour
Olive oil

Mix together pork, pepper, garlic powder, salt, egg, and parsley. Add enough bread crumbs to bind mixture together. Form mixture into 6 small rolls. Dredge rolls in flour. Fry in hot olive oil until golden brown and thoroughly cooked; drain. Makes 6 servings.

homemade chorizo

Use ⅓ cup mixture for each commercial link.

1 pound lean pork shoulder
2 tablespoons vinegar
1 teaspoon crushed oregano
1 garlic clove, mashed

½ teaspoon freshly ground
   black pepper
1 teaspoon salt
⅛ teaspoon cumin

Coarsely grind pork shoulder or chop in food processor. Add remaining ingredients. Mix thoroughly by hand. (Do not use mixer—meat will toughen.) Pack into crock or glass jar; refrigerate. Use within 1 week. Makes 4 servings.

chick-peas with garlic sausage
basque garbanzos con chorizo

This meal must be planned ahead; you need to soak the chick-peas the day before you prepare the dish.

2 cups dried chick-peas
1 pound chorizos or other
   garlic-flavored sausage
2 tablespoons olive oil
1 large Spanish onion,
   chopped

2 garlic cloves, minced
1 large green pepper, seeded,
   sliced into strips
1½ cups tomato sauce
1 teaspoon salt

Wash chick-peas; place in large Dutch oven. Cover with cold water; soak overnight. Next day bring chick-peas to boil. Reduce heat to simmer; cook 2 hours or until tender, but still retain their shape.

Prick sausage with fork. Place in shallow skillet; cover with cold water. Bring water to boil. Boil sausage 5 minutes; drain. Slice into ¼-inch slices.

Heat oil. Fry sausage until brown. Remove from oil. Add onion and garlic; sauté 8 minutes. Add pepper; sauté until peppers are limp but still crisp. Add chick-peas, sausage, tomato sauce, and salt to skillet; stir. Simmer 15 minutes or until thoroughly heated. Makes 8 servings.

fried potatoes with garlic sausage
papas frita con chorizos

A delicious late-evening supper served with wine and hard rolls.

1 pound chorizos or other
   garlic-flavored sausage
2 tablespoons olive oil
4 large potatoes, peeled, sliced
   thin

1 tablespoon chopped fresh
   parsley

Pierce sausage with fork. Place in shallow skillet; cover with water. Bring to boil; reduce heat. Cook 5 minutes; drain. Peel skin from sausage; slice into ½-inch-thick slices.

Heat oil in large skillet until haze forms above oil. Add sausage; brown evenly on both sides. Remove sausage from skillet; reserve.

Add potatoes to skillet. Spread evenly over bottom of skillet. Fry over medium heat on one side without stirring, about 12 minutes. When done on one side, use pancake turner and flip potatoes with one turn. Fry remaining side of potatoes until done.

To serve, garnish with fried sausage and parsley. Makes 4 servings.

tripe stew

A gourmet dish saved for company.

1 pound chorizos or garlic-
  flavored sausage
½ pound Serrano or smoked
  ham
½ cup olive oil
1 1-pound can tripe
½ cup all-purpose flour
1½ quarts beef broth
½ teaspoon salt
½ teaspoon celery salt
½ teaspoon onion powder

¼ teaspoon thyme
3 peppercorns
½ teaspoon crushed oregano
1 bay leaf
1 cup Spanish onions,
  chopped coarsely
4 carrots
4 potatoes
¼ cup flour
⅓ cup cold water
3 tablespoons tomato paste

Pierce sausage with fork. Place in shallow skillet; cover with water.
Bring to boil; reduce heat. Cook 5 minutes; drain. Peel skin from
sausage; slice into ½-inch-thick slices.

Chop ham into small cubes.

Heat ¼ cup oil in skillet. Fry sausage until brown on each side. Remove
sausage from skillet. Add ham; brown. Remove from skillet; reserve
meat and remaining frying oil.

Remove gelatin from tripe; reserve. Wash tripe; drain well. Coat with ½
cup flour.

Add ¼ cup oil to frying skillet. Heat until hot. Add coated tripe; fry until
well-browned. Remove tripe from skillet; place in large Dutch oven. Add
reserved gelatin, beef broth, salt, celery salt, onion powder, thyme,
peppercorns, oregano, bay leaf, and onions. Bring to boil. Cover; simmer
45 minutes.

While tripe is cooking, peel and dice carrots and potatoes. Cover
vegetables with water; simmer until tender but not mushy.

Drain broth from tripe. Remove bay leaf and peppercorns. Measure out
2¼ cups broth. If broth is short, add vegetable liquid to obtain 2¼ cups
liquid. Reheat.

Form paste with ¼ cup flour and cold water. Slowly stir flour paste into
heated stock; stir until stock thickens.

Add tomato paste, sausage, ham, and vegetables to tripe. Mix just
enough to blend. Pour thickened stock over tripe mixture. Reheat. Serve
immediately. Makes 6 servings.

veal and sour cream with rice
carne de ternera y jocoqui con arroz

2 tablespoons olive oil
1¼ pounds veal cubes
1 Spanish onion, chopped
1 green pepper, seeded,
  chopped
1 teaspoon garlic powder
¼ teaspoon pepper

1 teaspoon paprika
1 teaspoon salt
3 cups beef broth, boiling
1 cup long-grain rice
2 tablespoons snipped fresh
  parsley
1 cup sour cream

Heat oil until haze forms above pan. Reduce heat; brown veal in oil. Add
vegetables and seasonings; sauté until limp. Add broth; simmer 20
minutes. Add rice and parsley; stir; bring to boil; reduce heat. Cover;
cook 20 minutes or until rice has absorbed all liquid. Stir in sour cream.
Reheat. Serve immediately. Makes 4 to 6 servings.

pork fillets
carne de cerdo

2 pounds pork tenderloin
1 large apple
2 tablespoons chopped
almonds
1 teaspoon sugar
¼ teaspoon cinnamon
¼ teaspoon garlic powder
1 teaspoon salt
¼ teaspoon freshly ground
pepper
¼ cup olive oil
½ cup dry red wine
1 cup stock

Slice tenderloin into 6 pieces.

Peel, core, and finely chop apple. Combine apple, almonds, sugar, and cinnamon; mix well.

Make slash in center of each tenderloin. Stuff with apple filling. Press meat together; secure with metal clamps if necessary.

Combine garlic powder, salt, and pepper. Rub tenderloins with mixture.

Heat oil in deep skillet. Brown tenderloins on all sides. Add wine and stock; bring to boil. Reduce heat; simmer 1 hour, turning meat at 15-minute intervals.

These are generally served with a tossed salad and mashed potatoes. Makes 4 servings.

pork fillets

boiled beef

boiled beef
cocido

2 cups navy beans or chick-
    peas
¼ cup olive oil
4 chicken backs, necks, and
    wings
3-pound chuck roast
2 to 3 cups water
2 onions

4 carrots
4 parsnips
4 potatoes
1 tablespoon salt
2 to 3 peppercorns
1 bay leaf
Fried Garlic Croutons (see
    Index)

Cover beans with water. Soak overnight; drain.

Heat oil in large Dutch oven. Add chicken and roast; fry until browned.
Add beans. Add enough water to cover meat and beans; heat to boiling.
Reduce heat to simmer; cook 2½ to 3 hours.

While meat and beans are simmering, clean and slice vegetables. Add
vegetables and spices to stew. Simmer 1 to 2 hours or until meat is tender
and falls apart when touched.

To serve, ladle broth into soup bowls; serve with croutons. Next serve
vegetables. As the finale, serve the meat with Garlic Mayonnaise (see
Index) or Almond and Hot Pepper Sauce (see Index). Makes 6 to 8
servings.

44

veal kidneys
in claret
rinones al jerez

6 veal kidneys
3 tablespoons butter
1 clove garlic, chopped
2 medium onions, thinly sliced
1 pound fresh mushrooms,
   cleaned, sliced
3 tablespoons flour
1 cup chicken stock
1 cup claret
1 tablespoon parsley
1 teaspoon salt
Dash of pepper

Split and clean kidneys; remove skin and tissue. Soak in ice-cold water ½ hour. Heat oven to 350°F. Cut kidneys into ½-inch slices.

Melt butter in shallow skillet. Add garlic. Sauté kidneys in garlic butter 5 minutes. Remove kidneys; discard garlic. Add onions and mushrooms. Sauté until limp. Remove vegetables.

Add flour to skillet; stir to form paste. Add liquids; bring to boil. Add seasonings. Layer kidneys and vegetables in buttered 2½-quart casserole. Cover with sauce. Cover tightly; bake at 350°F 30 minutes or until tender. Serve over Saffron Rice (see Index). Makes 4 servings.

rabbit in
chilindron sauce
conejo en
salsa chilindron

Spanish people use a substantial amount of game in their daily menus.

1 medium-size rabbit
2 tablespoons olive oil
1 recipe Chilindron Sauce (see
   Index)
1 cup sliced pimiento-stuffed
   green olives

Cut rabbit into serving pieces. Wash; pat dry.

Heat oil in deep skillet. Brown rabbit evenly on all sides. Remove rabbit from skillet.

Prepare sauce as directed in pan used to fry rabbit, or, if sauce is made ahead of time, reheat in same skillet. Add rabbit to heated sauce. Coat rabbit with sauce; reduce heat. Cover pan; simmer 1 hour or until rabbit is tender.

To serve, spoon into serving dish; garnish with olives. Makes 4 servings.

chicken

chicken
bread pies
empanada gallega

3 tablespoons olive oil
½ cup chopped onion
½ cup chopped green pepper
½ cup chopped Serrano ham
1½ cups peeled, chopped
   tomatoes
½ cup chick-peas
½ teaspoon garlic powder
½ teaspoon salt
Dash of cayenne
1 box hot-roll mix
1 cup warm water
1 egg, beaten
1 egg white, unbeaten

Heat oil in skillet. Add onion and green pepper; sauté until tender. Add ham, tomatoes, chick-peas, garlic powder, salt, and cayenne. Simmer until mixture thickens and holds its shape in spoon.

Dissolve yeast from hot-roll mix in warm water as directed on package. Add beaten egg; blend well. Add flour mixture to yeast mixture; blend well. Cover; let rise in warm place until double in bulk.

Punch down dough; place on well-floured surface. Roll out to 16 × 20-inch rectangle. Cut into 4-inch squares. Fill each square with heaping tablespoon of chicken mixture. Bring corners together; pinch edges together. Place on greased cookie sheet, pinched-edges-down. Let rise 30 minutes. Brush with egg white. Bake at 350°F 30 minutes. Makes 6 servings.

Picture on opposite page: chicken canalones

chicken canalones

Pasta dishes are generally associated with Italian cooking; however, the Spanish diet contains many pasta favorites.

canalone dough

3 cups all-purpose flour
½ teaspoon salt
3 eggs
2 tablespoons olive oil
5 tablespoons water

Sift flour and salt into large bowl. Make well in center. Add remaining ingredients; blend together, using pastry blender. When dough forms into ball, knead 5 minutes. Cover dough; let rest 5 minutes. Roll dough out on floured surface into 16 4½ × 5-inch paper-thin rectangles.

chicken filling

2 garlic cloves, minced
2 onions, chopped fine
1 pound cooked chicken,
  diced
2 tablespoons tomato paste
½ cup dry red wine
1 tablespoon snipped fresh
  parsley
1 teaspoon salt
Dash of black pepper
1 teaspoon oregano

Mix together ingredients. Place some of filling in center of each pasta rectangle. Roll firmly; seal seams and ends, moistening with water to fasten.

Drop filled pasta into boiling salted water; cook 10 minutes. Remove with slotted spoon; place seam-side-down in greased shallow baking dish.

sauce

¼ cup olive oil
1 onion, chopped
2 garlic cloves, minced
1 green pepper, seeded,
  chopped
1 cup tomato sauce
¼ cup tomato paste
3 tablespoons dry red wine
1 teaspoon salt
Dash of pepper
1 tablespoon sugar

garnish

¼ cup Parmesan cheese

Heat oil. Add vegetables; sauté until limp. Add remaining ingredients; cook 20 minutes or until mixture thickens and holds its shape in spoon. Spread sauce over pasta. Garnish with Parmesan cheese. Bake in 400°F oven 15 minutes. Makes 4 to 6 servings.

chicken with peppers, tomatoes, and olives
pollo a la chilindron

With a few changes to the original method of preparation, this is an easy dish to prepare.

3 cups cooked chicken or
  turkey
2 large onions
1 red sweet pepper
1 green pepper
½ cup tomato sauce
1 tablespoon tomato paste
1 16-ounce can stewed
  tomatoes
1 teaspoon salt
½ teaspoon garlic powder
¼ teaspoon pepper
10 pitted black olives, sliced
10 pitted green olives, sliced

Cut chicken into slices.

Peel and slice onions.

Core, remove seeds, and slice peppers into strips.

Layer chicken, onions, and peppers in greased baking dish.

Combine tomato sauce, tomato paste, tomatoes, salt, garlic powder, and pepper in saucepan. Heat to boiling. Pour sauce over layered chicken and vegetables; cover. Bake in 350°F oven 30 minutes. Uncover casserole; sprinkle with olives. Bake 15 minutes more. Makes 4 to 6 servings.

rice with chicken
arroz con pollo

2 chicken breasts
3 chicken legs and thighs
½ cup olive oil
2 tablespoons sherry
½ cup chopped onions
1 green pepper, chopped
1 cup long-grain rice
1½ cups chicken broth,
  boiling
1 teaspoon garlic powder
1 bay leaf
½ teaspoon salt
¼ teaspoon pepper
Pinch of saffron
2 medium tomatoes, peeled,
  seeded, quartered
¼ cup freshly grated
  Parmesan cheese

Rinse chicken. Pat dry.

Heat oil in skillet until haze forms above skillet. Reduce heat; brown chicken well on all sides. Remove chicken from pan; drizzle with sherry.

Add vegetables to oil; cook until limp. Add rice; sauté until opaque and well-coated with oil. Add boiling chicken broth and seasonings; return to boil.

Pour rice mixture into 2½-quart greased casserole. Top with browned chicken. Cover; bake in 350°F oven 45 minutes. Place tomato quarters on top of chicken. Sprinkle with Parmesan cheese. Bake 15 minutes. Makes 4 servings.

chicken cooked in foil
pollo en camisa

4 chicken quarters
¼ cup olive oil
1 teaspoon salt
¼ teaspoon pepper
1 teaspoon garlic powder
1 small Spanish onion, chopped
½ cup finely chopped green pepper
2 teaspoons dried parsley
2 fresh tomatoes, peeled, chopped

Rinse chicken; pat dry with paper towel.

Cut 4 10-inch squares of heavy-duty foil. Pour 1 tablespoon oil on each sheet of foil; spread to cover foil. Place chicken on foil squares. Sprinkle with salt, pepper, and garlic powder.

Combine onion, green pepper, parsley, and tomatoes; toss. Spoon vegetable mixture evenly over chicken quarters. Fold and seal foil. Place foil packs on cookie sheet; bake at 425°F 40 minutes.

Serve chicken from foil packets. Be careful when opening packets: Steam is trapped inside. Makes 4 servings.

chicken seville style

¼ cup olive oil
3 chicken legs and thighs
1 Spanish onion, peeled, sliced
½ cup diced Serrano or other smoked ham
1 tablespoon tomato paste
2 cans stewed tomatoes
1 teaspoon garlic powder
1 teaspoon salt
¼ teaspoon pepper
¼ teaspoon thyme
¼ cup sliced pitted black olives
¼ cup sliced stuffed Spanish olives

In large, deep skillet, heat oil until haze forms above skillet; reduce heat. Add chicken pieces; brown evenly on all sides. Remove chicken.

Add onion and ham to skillet; cook until onion slices wilt and ham begins to brown, about 5 minutes. Drain excess oil from skillet. Add chicken, tomato paste, tomatoes, and spices. Turn heat to high; cook until mixture boils. Reduce heat to simmer; cover. Cook 30 minutes or until chicken is fork-tender; uncover. Add olives; cook 5 minutes.

Serve chicken from skillet. Makes 4 servings.

chicken cooked in foil

paella

6 rock lobster tails
12 large raw shrimp
6 cherrystone clams
6 mussels
½ pound chorizos or other garlic-flavored sausage
⅔ cup olive oil
½ pound pork cubes
4 chicken breasts, thighs, and legs
1 onion
1 green pepper
¼ cup tomato sauce
3 cups long-grain rice
⅛ teaspoon saffron powder
1 teaspoon salt
1 teaspoon garlic powder
¼ teaspoon pepper
1½ quarts boiling water
1 cup frozen peas
1 fresh tomato, peeled, seeded, diced

With kitchen shears, break center of ribs on belly side of lobster shell. Loosen meat from shell with fingers, leaving meat attached near tail fins.

Shell and devein shrimp.

Scrub clams and mussels.

Soak mussels in cold water 30 minutes to remove salty taste. Discard any that open their shells while soaking; drain.

Place sausage in shallow skillet. Cover with water; bring to boil. Boil 5 minutes; drain. Remove skin from sausage; cut into ¼-inch rounds.

Heat ⅓ cup oil. Fry sausage until browned on each side. Remove from skillet; drain.

Add pork to heated oil. Fry until brown on all sides and no longer pink. Remove from skillet; drain.

Add chicken to skillet. Fry 45 minutes or until golden brown and meat is cooked. Remove from skillet; drain.

Add lobster to skillet; fry just until shells start to turn pink. Remove from skillet; drain.

Add remaining oil to skillet; heat thoroughly.

Peel and chop onion. Sauté in skillet 10 minutes or until tender.

Remove seeds and membranes from pepper; dice. Add to onions; sauté 5 minutes. Stir in tomato sauce; simmer until mixture thickens and holds its shape in spoon. Add rice, saffron, salt, garlic powder, and pepper; mix well. Add boiling water; mix well. Bring mixture to boil; reduce heat to simmer.

Arrange lobster, shrimp, clams, mussels, sausage, pork, and chicken on top of rice mixture. Scatter peas and tomato over rice and meat; cover.

Simmer 30 to 45 minutes or until rice is tender, shrimp and lobster meat turns white, and mussels and clams pop open. Remove from heat. Cover; let rest 10 minutes for flavors to mingle.

Serve paella directly from pan. Makes 6 to 8 servings.

paella

Paella is known as the dish of Spain. Dine anywhere in Spain, from a gourmet restaurant to a countryside picnic, and you will find Paella being prepared.

The traditional way to serve paella is to place the cooking pan (paella pan) in the center of the dining table with a large soup bowl inverted over the center of the pan. On top of this bowl is placed a salad composed

paella

largely of lettuce wedges, quartered tomatoes, and large chunks of onion.

Each guest serves himself from the paella pan. When he needs a light refresher to go with his paella, he spears a piece of salad and eats it from his fork.

The purpose of the soup bowl is to keep the center portion warm for those who want second or third portions.

traditional fried crullers

king's bread ring

breads

king's bread ring
rosca de reyes

2 packages active dry yeast
1 cup warm milk
⅓ cup sugar
⅓ cup margarine
2 teaspoons salt
1½ teaspoons freshly grated
  orange peel
3 eggs, well beaten
4 to 4½ cups all-purpose flour
¼ cup margarine, melted

rum icing

1⅓ cups powdered sugar
1 to 2 tablespoons milk
1 teaspoon rum flavoring

candied-fruit topping

5 candied cherries, chopped
10 candied orange peel strips

Sprinkle yeast on milk; stir to dissolve.

Cream sugar and ⅓ cup margarine. Blend in salt and orange peel. Add 1 egg, yeast mixture, and enough flour to make stiff dough. Turn out on lightly floured surface; knead until smooth and elastic, about 10 minutes. Place in greased bowl; grease top. Cover; let rise until double in bulk. Punch down.

Knead until smooth, about 2 minutes. Roll dough into long rope; place on greased cookie sheet. Shape into ring, sealing ends together. Push a coin into dough so it is completely covered. Brush with ¼ cup margarine. Cover; let rise until double in bulk, about 1½ hours. Bake at 375°F 30 minutes or until golden brown; cool.

Combine powdered sugar, milk, and rum flavoring. Beat until smooth.

Frost bread with icing; decorate with candied fruit as illustrated. Makes 12 servings.

traditional fried crullers

churros

Oil for deep frying
½ lime
1 cup water
1 10-ounce package pie-crust
  mix

3 eggs
Powdered sugar

Heat oil to 370°F in large, heavy skillet. Oil should be 3 inches deep and pan no more than half full. Add lime.

Bring water to boil. Quickly stir in pie-crust mix; stir until mixture forms ball and leaves sides of pan. Transfer dough to pastry bag fitted with star tip.

Remove lime from fat.

Squeeze dough into hot fat in continuous spiral to fill pan. Do not crowd. Cook until golden brown, turning once during cooking process; drain.

Dust with powdered sugar. Serve immediately. Makes 6 servings.

cinnamon muffins

1½ cups all-purpose flour
1½ teaspoons baking powder
¼ teaspoon salt
½ teaspoon cinnamon
5 tablespoons butter, room
  temperature

½ cup sugar
1 egg
½ cup milk

Sift together flour, baking powder, salt, and cinnamon.

Cream butter until fluffy. Beat in sugar; beat until creamy. Add egg; beat well. Stir in dry ingredients alternately with milk; stir just enough to mix. Spoon batter into greased muffin tins. Bake in preheated 400°F oven 30 minutes.

Serve muffins warm. Makes 1 dozen.

continental rolls

rollos de continente

1 cake compressed yeast
2 cups warm water
1 tablespoon sugar

2 teaspoons salt
5 to 6 cups flour
1 egg white, unbeaten

Crumble yeast over water. Stir until dissolved. Add sugar, salt, and 3 cups of flour. Stir to mix; beat until smooth. Work in 2¼ cups more flour with your hands. Sprinkle some of remaining flour over flat surface. Turn dough onto floured surface; knead until smooth, about 10 minutes. If dough sticks to surface, add more flour. Shape dough into smooth ball. Place ball in greased bowl; grease top. Cover; let rise until doubled in bulk. Punch down.

Form rolls by pinching off pieces of dough size of an egg. Shape into smooth roll. Place on greased cookie sheet.

With scissors make cross-shaped gash ½ inch deep in top of each roll. Cover; let rise until double in bulk. Bake in 425°F oven in which shallow pan of boiling water has been placed on floor of oven. Bake 20 minutes. Remove from oven; brush with egg white. Return to oven 2 minutes. Makes 2 dozen rolls.

continental bread
pan de continente

1 package active dry yeast
2 cups warm water
1 tablespoon sugar
1½ teaspoons salt
5 to 6 cups flour
Cornmeal
1 egg white, unbeaten

Stir yeast in water until dissolved. Add sugar, salt, and 3 cups flour. Stir to mix; beat until smooth. Work in 2¼ cups more flour with your hands.

Sprinkle some of remaining flour over flat surface. Turn dough onto floured surface; knead until smooth, about 10 minutes. If dough sticks to surface, add more flour. Shape dough into smooth ball. Place ball in greased bowl; grease top. Cover; let rise until double in bulk. Punch down.

Turn the dough onto lightly floured board. Divide into 2 equal portions. Roll each portion into 15 × 10-inch oblong. Beginning at widest side, roll dough up tightly. Pinch edges together. Taper ends by gently rolling dough back and forth. Place loaves on greased baking sheets sprinkled with cornmeal. Cover; let rise in a warm place about 1 hour or until doubled in bulk.

With sharp razor make diagonal cuts on top of each loaf. Brush with unbeaten egg white. Place loaves in cold oven in which pan of boiling water has been placed. Set oven at 450°F; bake loaves about 35 minutes or until golden crust has formed. Remove from oven; cool on wire rack. Makes 2 loaves.

holiday fruit bread
pan dulce de frutas

3 teaspoons baking powder
½ teaspoon salt
¾ cup granulated sugar
¾ cup butter
1½ cups chopped candied
    fruit
1½ cups all-purpose flour
½ cup raisins
2 eggs, beaten
1 tablespoon light rum

Sift flour, baking powder, salt, and sugar together into mixing bowl. Cut in butter until mixture resembles fine bread crumbs. Stir in fruit. Add eggs and rum; mix well. Spread batter into greased loaf pan. Bake in 325°F oven 60 minutes or until done. Cool slightly; remove from pan.

rum glaze

1¼ cups powdered sugar
3½ tablespoons rum

Combine sugar and rum; stir to form smooth icing. Drizzle over warm cake. Cool before cutting. Makes 1 9-inch loaf.

saffron almond braid

1 package active dry yeast
¾ cup warm water
1 cup all-purpose flour
¼ cup sugar
¼ cup olive oil or melted
  butter
1 teaspoon salt
⅛ teaspoon saffron
1 egg, beaten
3 to 4 cups all-purpose flour
1½ cups blanched whole
  almonds
¾ cup white raisins
Melted butter
Coarse sugar crystals

Dissolve yeast in water. Stir in flour and sugar. Let stand covered in warm place 1 hour to allow yeast to work.

Add sugar, oil, salt, saffron, and egg; mix. Add 1 cup flour to sponge; mix well. Pour 1 cup flour on top of kneading surface. Pour sponge mixture on top of flour. Cover sponge with ½ cup flour. Knead until flour is worked into dough. Add almonds and raisins; work in. Continue adding flour until soft dough is formed. Knead dough 10 minutes or until folds form in dough. Place in greased bowl; grease top. Cover; let rise until double in bulk. Punch down.

Divide dough into 3 pieces. Roll each piece into 15-inch-long rope. Lay each rope 1 inch apart on greased cookie sheet. Braid by starting in center and working toward each end. Cover; let rise until doubled in bulk.

Bake at 375°F 30 minutes or until done. Brush with butter; sprinkle with sugar. Makes 1 braid.

spanish french toast
torrijas

Oil for frying
1 loaf Continental Bread (see
  Index)
2 eggs
1 teaspoon cinnamon
2 tablespoons water
1 cup sifted powdered sugar

Heat oil to 370°F in large, heavy saucepan.

Slice bread into 8 thick slices; discard ends. Cut 2 circles from each slice, using biscuit cutter.

Beat eggs until fluffy. Add cinnamon and water; mix well.

Dip both sides of each bread circle into egg mixture. Do not soak, or bread will fall apart. Fry in oil until light brown on each side. Remove from oil; drain on brown paper bag. Sift powdered sugar over each side. Serve immediately. Makes 16 torrijas.

desserts and beverage

soft custard
natillas

3 eggs
2 egg yolks
½ cup granulated sugar
3 cups milk

2 4-inch cinnamon sticks
6 ladyfingers
Whipped cream

Combine eggs, egg yolks, and sugar. Beat at medium speed with electric mixer 5 minutes or until mixture thickens.

Heat milk and cinnamon sticks slowly in heavy saucepan until mixture starts to bubble around edges. *Do not boil.* Remove cinnamon sticks.

Beating constantly, slowly pour hot milk into egg mixture in steady stream. Pour mixture into top of double boiler. Cook over boiling water, stirring constantly, 20 to 25 minutes or until thickened. Pour into serving dishes; cover with waxed paper. Refrigerate until cooled.

To serve, garnish each dish with a ladyfinger and whipped cream. Makes 6 servings.

mint apple crisp

½ cup granulated sugar
½ cup brown sugar
2 eggs, beaten
1 cup all-purpose flour
½ teaspoon salt
2 teaspoons baking powder
1 teaspoon cinnamon

1½ cups cooking apples, peeled, diced
1 teaspoon mint flavoring
½ cup chopped blanched almonds
1 cup table cream

Gradually add sugars to eggs; beat well. Add flour, salt, baking powder, and cinnamon. Fold in apples, mint flavoring, and nuts. Pour into greased 9 × 9-inch pan. Bake in 350°F oven 30 minutes.

Serve apple crisp warm with cream. Makes 6 servings.

honeyed apples
manzanas en dulce

4 medium cooking apples
¼ cup chopped blanched
  almonds
⅓ cup chopped dried figs
¼ cup butter
¼ cup honey

Core apples. Cut thin line through peeling around center of each apple. Place apples in baking dish.

Combine almonds and figs. Fill apple centers with fig and nut mixture. Place 1 tablespoon butter and honey in each apple center. Bake in 375°F oven 45 minutes or until apples are tender but still retain their shape. Baste occasionally with liquid that accumulates on bottom of pan. Remove apples from oven; gently slip top half of apple peel away.

Place apples in serving dish; spoon pan juice over apples. Serve warm. Makes 4 servings.

honeyed apples

strawberries in wine
fresas en vino

Fresh fruit is a popular dessert and/or snack in Spain.

24 large, freshly picked　　**1 cup dry white wine**
  strawberries　　　　　　　**Sugar**

Remove stems from strawberries; wash thoroughly. Place in shallow dish; cover with wine. Allow to marinate 3 to 4 hours in refrigerator.

Remove strawberries from wine (save wine for a punch); arrange on serving tray. Place small bowl of sugar on tray to allow guests to coat strawberries with sugar if desired. Makes 4 to 6 servings.

coconut pudding
cocada

A special holiday treat.

8 egg yolks　　　　　　**1½ cups freshly grated**
1 cup sugar　　　　　　　**coconut**
½ cup flour　　　　　　　**1 teaspoon vanilla extract**
2 cups milk　　　　　　　**Chopped almonds**
½ cup dry white wine

Combine egg yolks, sugar, and flour. Beat until creamy.

Place milk and wine in double boiler. Heat to boiling. Pour milk mixture slowly into egg mixture, stirring constantly to prevent curdling. Add coconut and vanilla; mix well. Cook over double boiler until mixture thickens and coats wooden spoon. Cover top with waxed paper to prevent scum from forming. Cool in refrigerator.

To serve, spoon into serving dishes; sprinkle with chopped almonds. Makes 6 to 8 servings.

cinnamon flan

1 cup sugar
2 tablespoons water
4 eggs
1 14-ounce can sweetened
  condensed milk

1 cup water
½ teaspoon cinnamon
½ teaspoon grated lemon rind

Combine sugar and 2 tablespoons water in heavy, small skillet. Cook, stirring constantly, until caramelized and syrupy. Immediately pour into warm 4-cup buttered mold; tilt to coat bottom and sides of container while sugar is still hot.

Beat eggs well. Add milk, 1 cup water, cinnamon, and lemon peel; mix well. Pour into prepared mold. Place casserole in larger pan containing hot water to level of custard. Bake at 350°F 1 hour or until knife inserted in center comes out clean. Cool completely.

Loosen custard with knife; invert on serving platter. Spoon caramel over top. Makes 4 to 6 servings.

valencia crepes

4 eggs
1 cup flour
2 tablespoons sugar
1 cup milk
¼ cup water
1 tablespoon melted
  margarine
8 Valencia oranges

3 tablespoons kirsch
2 tablespoons Grand Marnier
1 cup sour cream
8 ounces cream cheese,
  softened
½ cup sugar
Powdered sugar for dusting

Beat eggs with whisk in medium mixing bowl. Gradually add flour and sugar alternately with milk and water, beating until smooth. Beat in margarine. Refrigerate 1 hour before using.

Prepare crepes.

Peel oranges. Cut into segments, cutting between membranes. Slice each segment into 3 to 4 pieces. Sprinkle oranges with kirsch and Grand Marnier.

Blend sour cream, cream cheese, and sugar. Fold oranges into cream mixture, saving ½ cup oranges for garnish. Top each crepe with 2 to 3 tablespoons cheese and orange mixture. Roll up.

Place crepes on serving platter. Dust with powdered sugar. Garnish with orange slices. Makes 6 servings.

valencia crepes

spanish wings
alas español

Delightful mild cookies, crisp enough for dunking with your favorite hot beverage.

⅓ cup shortening
⅔ cup sugar
1 tablespoon cold water
2 egg yolks
1 teaspoon freshly grated
  lemon peel

2 cups flour
¼ teaspoon salt
2 egg whites, unbeaten

Cream shortening and sugar until light and fluffy. Beat in water, egg yolks, and lemon peel. Work flour and salt in with your hands to form smooth dough. Wrap dough in waxed paper; chill.

Pinch off walnut-size piece of dough; roll it into 4- to 5-inch rope. Place on cookie sheet. Fold rope in middle, then fold each end back to meet fold in middle. Pinch together. Brush with egg whites. Bake at 325°F 10 minutes or until cookies just start to turn brown. Makes 4 dozen cookies.

fried custard squares
leche frita

1 cup all-purpose flour
3 cups milk
½ teaspoon cinnamon
½ cup granulated sugar
1 teaspoon vanilla

¼ cup butter*
1 egg, beaten
1 cup coffee-cake or sweet-
  bun crumbs

Pour flour into heavy saucepan. Slowly add 1 cup milk to form smooth paste. Add remaining milk, cinnamon, and sugar. Beat with electric mixer until smooth. Place mixture over heat. Cook on high until mixture boils and thickens. (Stir constantly while cooking, to prevent scorching.) When mixture thickens, remove from flame; beat in vanilla. Pour custard mixture into 8-inch-square cake pan. Chill 5 hours.

Remove custard from refrigerator; cut into 2-inch squares.

Melt butter in skillet.

Coat custard with egg, then with crumbs. Fry in butter until golden brown on both sides, about 40 seconds on each side. Serve hot. Makes 8 servings.

* Olive oil may be substituted if you prefer.

sangria

sangria

4 center orange slices, seeded
4 center lemon slices, seeded
1 cinnamon stick
⅓ cup sugar
2 ounces brandy
1 quart red dry Spanish wine
16 ounces club soda
Ice cubes

Combine orange slices, lemon slices, cinnamon stick, sugar, brandy, and wine. Cover; let stand 1 hour at room temperature.

Pour wine mixture and club soda over ice. Serve in ice-filled glasses. Makes 6 to 8 servings.

index

A

Almond
  and Pepper Sauce, Hot 9
  and Pepper Sauce, Mild 9
  Saffron Braid 58
  Soup 10
  Stuffed Olives 8
Andulusia Daily Soup 33
Apple Mint Crisp 59
Apples with Cabbage 23
Apples, Honeyed 60
Artichoke Hearts
  Shrimp with Vegetables 34
Asparagus, White, Steamed,
  with Garlic Mayonnaise 23

B

Baby Eels 5
Baked Fish 35
Baked Fresh Sardines 31
Bean Salad, Garbanzo 17
Bean and Sausage Soup 10
Beans
  Green, with Ham 21
  Green, in Tomato Sauce 21
  Lima, and Peppers 23
Beef
  Boiled 44
  Roast, Marinated 39
  Simmered in Wine 39
Beets, Pickled 7
Boiled
  Beef 44
  Potatoes with Garlic Mayonnaise 24
  Shrimp with Sauces 29
Braid, Saffron Almond 58
Bread
  Continental 57
  Fruit, Holiday 57
  Pies, Chicken 47
  Ring, King's 55
Broiled Fish 33

C

Cabbage with Apples 23
Canalone Dough 48
Canalones, Chicken 48
Candied-Fruit Topping 55
Cauliflower
  Pickled 7
  Shrimp with Vegetables 34
Cheese Mold 10
Chicken
  Bread Pies 47
  Canalones 49
  Cooked in Foil 50
  Filling 49
  Paella 51, 52
  with Peppers, Tomatoes,
    and Olives 49
  with Rice 49
  Seville Style 50
Chick-Pea Fritters 8
Chick-Peas with Garlic Sausage 41
Chilindron Sauce 9
  Rabbit in 45
Chorizos
  Chick-Peas with Garlic
    Sausage 41
  Fried Potatoes with Garlic
    Sausage 41
  Homemade 41
  Paella 51
  Tripe Stew 42
Chunky Tomato Sauce with
  Lettuce Wedge 17
Churros 56
Cinnamon Flan 61
Cinnamon Muffins 56
Clams
  Paella 51
Claret, Veal Kidneys in 45

Coconut Pudding 60
Cod Bake 31
Cod Fillets, Baked 35
Continental Bread 57
Continental Rolls 56
Cookies
  Spanish Wings 62
Crepes Valencia 61
Croutons, Fried Garlic 9
Crullers, Traditional Fried 56
Custard
  Cinnamon Flan 61
  Soft 59
  Squares, Fried 62

D

Daily Soup Andalusia 33
Dates with Ham 7
Dressing, Honey 19
Dressing, Salad 18

E

Eels, Baby 5
Eggs, Scrambled 13
Eggs with Sofrito 15

F

Filling, Chicken 48
Filling, Turnover 8
Fish
  Baked 35
  Broiled 33
  Fried, with Sour Sauce 32
  Pickled 6
  Soup, Andalusia Daily 33
  Steamed Galician, in Tomato
    Sauce 30
  Tuna, with Rice Salad 31
Flan, Cinnamon 61
French Toast Spanish 58
Fresh-Fruit Salad 19
Fried
  Crullers, Traditional 56
  Custard Squares 62
  Fish with Sour Sauce 32
  Garlic Croutons 9
  Potatoes with Garlic
    Sausage 41
Fritters, Chick-Pea 8
Fruit
  Bread, Holiday 57
  Salad, Fresh 19
  Topping, Candied 55

G

Galician Steamed Fish in
  Tomato Sauce 30
Garbanzo Bean Salad 17
Garden Casserole, Summer 25
Garlic Croutons, Fried 9
Garlic Mayonnaise 9
  Boiled Potatoes with 24
  Langostino with 5
  Steamed White Asparagus with 23
Garlic Sausage
  with Chick-Peas 41
  with Fried Potatoes 41
  Homemade 41
  Paella 51
  Tripe Stew 42
Garlic Soup 11
Gazpacho 12
  Quick 12
Galze, Rum 57
Green
  Beans with Ham 21
  Beans in Tomato Sauce 21
  Peppers and Onions 24

H

Haddock Fillets, Baked 35
Hake Fillets, Baked 35
Ham
  with Dates 7
  with Green Beans 21
  and Olive Turnovers 8
Holiday Fruit Bread 57

Homemade Chorizo 41
Hominy Soup 26
Honey Dressing 19
Honeyed Apples 60

I

Icing, Rum 55

K

Kidneys, Veal, in Claret 45
King's Bread Ring 55

L

Lamb Chops, Marinated 40
Lamb Chops Spanish 40
Langostino with Garlic
  Mayonnaise 5
Lettuce Wedge with Chunky
  Tomato Sauce 17
Lima Beans and Peppers 23
Lobster
  Paella 51
  and Shrimp Salad 35

M

Marinated Beef Roast 39
Marinated Lamb Chops 40
Mayonnaise, Garlic 9
  Boiled Potatoes with 24
  Langostino with 5
  Steamed White Asparagus with 23
Melon Salad 20
Mild Almond and Pepper Sauce 9
Mint Apple Crisp 59
Mixed Salad 18
Muffins, Cinnamon 56
Mussels
  Paella 51

O

Olive—Ham Turnovers 8
Olives, Almond-Stuffed 8
Olives, Peppers, and Tomatoes
  with Chicken 49
Omelet
  Onion and Potato 16
  Potato and Sausage 16
  with Sauce 15
  Supper 16
Omelets 15
Onion and Potato Omelet 16
Onions and Green Peppers 24
Oranges, Poached 20

P

Paella 51, 52
Parsley, Potatoes with 24
Pastry, Turnover 8
Pepper
  and Almond Sauce, Hot 9
  and Almond Sauce, Mild 9
  Pot 26
Peppers
  Green, and Onions 24
  and Lima Beans 23
  Tomatoes, and Olives
    with Chicken 49
Pickled
  Beets 7
  Cauliflower 7
  Fish 6
Poached Oranges 20
Pork
  Fillets 43
  Homemade Chorizo 41
  Paella 51
  Rolls 40
Potato and Onion Omelet 16
Potato and Sausage Omelet 16
Potatoes
  Boiled, with Garlic
    Mayonnaise 24
  Fried, with Garlic
    Sausage 41
  with Parsley 24
Pudding, Coconut 60

Q

Quick Gazpacho   12

R

Rabbit in Chilindron Sauce   45
Rice
   with Chicken   49
   Paella   51
   Saffron   26
   and Seafood   34
   Spanish   25
   with Tuna Fish
     Salad   31
   with Veal and Sour
     Cream   42
Roast Beef, Marinated   39
Rolls, Continental   56
Rum Glaze   57
Rum Icing   55

S

Saffron Almond Braid   58
Saffron Rice   26
Salad
   Fresh-Fruit   19
   Garbanzo Bean   17
   Lettuce Wedge with Chunky
     Tomato Sauce   17
   Melon   20
   Mixed   18
   Scalded   18
   Shrimp and Lobster   35
   Tossed   18
   Tuna Fish with Rice   31
Salad Dressing   18
Sangria   62
Sardines, Baked Fresh   31
Sauce   15, 48
   Almond and Pepper   9
   Chilindron   9
   Chilindron, Rabbit in   45
   Sour, Fried Fish with   32
Sauce, Tomato
   Chunky   17
   Galician Steamed Fish in   30
   Green Beans in   21

Sausage
   and Bean Soup   10
   Homemade Chorizo   41
   and Potato Omelet   16
Sausage, Garlic
   with Chick-Peas   41
   with Fried Potatoes   41
   Homemade   41
   Paella   51
   Tripe Stew   42
Scalded Salad   18
Scrambled Eggs   13
Seafood and Rice   34
Seville-Style Chicken   50
Shrimp
   Boiled, with Sauces   29
   and Lobster Salad   35
   Paella   51
   Seafood and Rice   34
   with Vegetables   34
Sofrito, Eggs with   15
Soft Custard   59
Soup
   Almond   10
   Andalusia Daily   33
   Bean and Sausage   10
   Garlic   11
   Gazpacho   12
   Gazpacho, Quick   12
   Hominy   26
Sour Cream and Veal
   with Rice   42
Sour Sauce, Fried
   Fish with   32
Spanish
   French Toast   58
   Lamb Chops   40
   Rice   25
   Wings   62
Steamed Fish Galician
   in Tomato Sauce   30
Steamed White Asparagus
   with Garlic Mayonnaise   23
Stew, Tripe   42
Stew, Tuna   32

Strawberries in Wine   60
Stuffed Olives, Almond   8
Summer Garden Casserole   25
Supper Omelet   16

T

Tomato Sauce
   Chunky   17
   Galician Steamed Fish
     in   30
   Green Beans in   21
Tomatoes, Peppers, and Olives
   with Chicken   49
Topping, Candied-Fruit   55
Tossed Salad   18
Traditional Fried Crullers   56
Tripe Stew   42
Tuna
   Fish with Rice Salad   31
   Stew   32
   Turnovers   8
Turnover Filling   8
Turnover Pastry   8
Turnovers, Olive—Ham   8
Turnovers, Tuna   8

V

Valencia Crepes   61
Veal Kidneys in Claret   45
Veal and Sour Cream
   with Rice   42
Vegetables with Shrimp   34

W

White Asparagus, Steamed, with
   Garlic Mayonnaise   23
Whitefish Fillets
   Fried Fish with Sour
     Sauce   32
   Galician Steamed Fish
     in Tomato Sauce   30
Wine, Beef Simmered
   in   39
Wine, Strawberries in   60
Wings Spanish   62